P&A MEDIA

Decisions for Generation Z

How to choose in a world of many options

First published by P&A Media 2024

Copyright © 2024 by P&A Media

All rights reserved. No part of this publication may be reproduced, stored or transmitted in any form or by any means, electronic, mechanical, photocopying, recording, scanning, or otherwise without written permission from the publisher. It is illegal to copy this book, post it to a website, or distribute it by any other means without permission.

P&A Media asserts the moral right to be identified as the author of this work.

P&A Media has no responsibility for the persistence or accuracy of URLs for external or third-party Internet Websites referred to in this publication and does not guarantee that any content on such Websites is, or will remain, accurate or appropriate.

Designations used by companies to distinguish their products are often claimed as trademarks. All brand names and product names used in this book and on its cover are trade names, service marks, trademarks and registered trademarks of their respective owners. The publishers and the book are not associated with any product or vendor mentioned in this book. None of the companies referenced within the book have endorsed the book.

First edition

This book was professionally typeset on Reedsy.
Find out more at reedsy.com

Contents

Introduction	1
1 The Power of taking a decisions	3
2 Which decisions are very important	6
Parents	6
School	7
Friends	7
Hobby	7
Self-Worth	8
Social Media	8
Relationship	8
Finance	9
Work Environment	9
Ethics and environmental sustainability	10
Conclusion	11
3 The process of decision making	12
Tips and Tricks on How to Make Decisions	14
Daily Decision	16
Power of Habits	16
Thinking Outside the Box	17
4 Obstacles	19
Overcoming the Paralysis of Infinite Choice Online	20
Techniques to Enhance Focus and Productivity:	21
Escaping the Comparison Trap	22

		Lifelong Learning	23
		Privacy in the Digital Age - Safeguarding Your Online Identity	23
		Conclusion	26
5		How to communicate your decision	27
		Communicating Decisions to Yourself:	27
		Communicating Decisions to Others:	29
		Conclusion	30
6		Conclusion	31

Introduction

When I stood at the Gate, ready to board the plane, I started to realize more and more the consequences of my decision. My decision was to leave the country and not coming back. Right, a one way ticket. Yes, this was a decision that I took many months ago, but in this moment of boarding the plane it came to reality and I could feel how I felt a mixture of emotions, of joy and excitement as well as sadness and fear. However, I never questioned my decision. I was simply sure.

And that's the aim of this book. That you are able to choose wisely and then go your way, comes whatever might come. You have chosen and decided and you will stick with it.

Especially in a world filled with endless possibilities and countless choices, the ability to make decisions is a skill that holds immense power. "Decisions for Generation Z: How to Choose in a World of Many Options" is a guidebook designed to empower you as a young individual to navigate the complexities of decision-making in today's fast-paced society.

This book explores the transformative potential of taking decisions and the impact it can have on shaping one's life. From understanding the decision-making process to overcoming indecision and fear, each chapter delves into practical strategies and insights to help readers make informed choices aligned with their values and goals.

Through real-life examples, actionable tips, and thought-provoking statements, "Decisions for Generation Z" equips readers with the tools they need to confidently navigate the myriad options before them. Whether facing major life transitions, career dilemmas, or personal challenges, this book serves as a roadmap for harnessing the power of decision-making to create a life that is authentic, purposeful, and fulfilling.

1

The Power of taking a decisions

In life, we are constantly faced with choices and decisions that shape our present and future. Some decisions may seem small and inconsequential, while others can have a profound impact on our lives. The power of taking decisions lies in the ability to take control of our destiny, shape our own path, and create the life we desire.

One of the key aspects of decision-making is the element of empowerment. When we make a decision, we are taking ownership of our actions and accepting responsibility for the outcomes. This sense of empowerment can be incredibly liberating, as it allows us to break free from indecision and passivity, and instead become active participants in our own lives.

Coming back to my experience at the gate, I could literally feel the weight and power of that decision in the past. It gave me the power to overcome the sadness of the separation of my family. It gave me the power to prepare for my new life. It gave my power to leave behind what had to be left behind, even if there was and still is value in it. That decision gave me the strength to overcome fear and doubts of an unsure future. Indeed, the decision to board that flight clarified every priority.

Taking decisions also helps us to clarify our values and priorities. By making choices based on what truly matters to us, we are able to align our actions with our beliefs and goals. This alignment brings a sense of purpose and direction to our lives, guiding us towards fulfillment and satisfaction.

Moreover, the power of taking decisions lies in its ability to propel us forward towards growth and progress. Every decision we make is an opportunity for learning and personal development. Whether we succeed or fail, each choice teaches us valuable lessons that help us evolve as individuals and navigate future challenges with greater wisdom and resilience.

Decisions also have the power to shape our relationships with others. The choices we make can strengthen bonds with loved ones, build trust and respect, or even lead to new connections and opportunities. By being intentional in our decision-making process, we can nurture positive interactions and create a supportive network that enriches our lives.

Furthermore, taking decisions is an act of courage. It requires us to step out of our comfort zones, confront uncertainty, and embrace change. By facing these challenges head-on, we demonstrate resilience, adaptability, and a willingness to take risks in pursuit of our dreams.

In essence, the power of taking decisions lies in its transformative potential. Each choice we make has the power to shape not only our individual paths but also the world around us. By embracing this power with intentionality and mindfulness, we can harness the full potential of decision-making to create a life that is meaningful, fulfilling, and true to who we are.

The power of making decisions is a fundamental aspect of human agency that empowers us to shape our destinies, clarify our values, foster personal growth, strengthen relationships, demonstrate courage, and effect positive change in the world. So next time you are faced with a choice, remember the immense power you hold in your hands – the power to decide your own fate.

2

Which decisions are very important

In this chapter, we will look at and discuss ten very important and crucial decisions. There are many choices. Some are big and quite a few are small, seemingly insignificant decisions. But every decision you make today defines who you will be tomorrow. And the following subtitles determine to a very strong degree who you are and what you will become in the future.

Parents

The relationship with parents is one of the most significant aspects of a person's life, and decisions made in this area can have a lasting impact. From communication and boundaries to conflict resolution and independence, navigating the parent-child dynamic requires thoughtful decision-making. Understanding and addressing issues within this relationship can lead to personal growth, improved family dynamics, and emotional well-being.

School

Education plays a crucial role in shaping one's future, making decisions related to school vital. Choosing subjects, extracurricular activities, career paths, and further education options are all key decisions that can influence academic success and career opportunities. Making informed choices in this area can lead to personal fulfillment, professional growth, and lifelong learning.

Friends

Friendships are an essential part of life, impacting our social support network, emotional well-being, and personal development. Decisions regarding friendships involve choosing who to spend time with, how to nurture relationships, and when to set boundaries. Cultivating healthy friendships based on mutual respect, trust, and shared values can enhance happiness, reduce stress, and foster a sense of belonging.

Hobby

Engaging in hobbies and interests is crucial for relaxation, creativity, and personal fulfillment. Deciding which hobbies to pursue, how to allocate time for them, and when to explore new interests are all important decisions that contribute to overall well-being. Hobbies provide an outlet for self-expression, stress relief, and skill development, enriching life outside of work or school.

Self-Worth

Self-worth encompasses how we perceive ourselves, our value system, and our sense of self-esteem. Making decisions that prioritize self-care, self-compassion, and self-improvement is essential for cultivating a positive self-image and inner confidence. Recognizing one's worth and making choices that honor personal boundaries and values are fundamental for mental health and overall happiness.

Social Media

In today's digital age, social media plays a significant role in how we connect with others, consume information, and present ourselves online. Decisions regarding social media usage, content sharing, privacy settings, and online interactions can impact mental health, relationships, and self-image. Being mindful of the influence of social media on our lives and making intentional choices about its role can lead to a healthier relationship with technology.

Relationship

Decisions related to romantic relationships involve choosing partners who align with our values, communication styles, and long-term goals. Setting boundaries, resolving conflicts constructively, and nurturing emotional intimacy require thoughtful decision-making skills. Building healthy relationships based on trust, respect, and mutual support can lead to greater emotional fulfillment and personal growth.

Finance

Managing finances effectively is crucial for long-term stability, security, and freedom. Decisions about budgeting, saving habits, investments, and debt management impact financial well-being and future goals.

Developing financial literacy, setting financial goals, and making informed choices about spending and saving are essential for achieving financial independence and building wealth over time.

Work Environment

As Generation Z enters the workforce, they are faced with a myriad of choices when it comes to selecting their preferred work environment. With options ranging from the private sector to state employment and the Gig Economy, young professionals must carefully consider their priorities and values before making a decision. In the private sector, Generation Z individuals are often attracted to the potential for career advancement, competitive salaries, and opportunities for skill development. Companies in this sector typically offer structured career paths, mentorship programs, and a corporate culture that values innovation and creativity. However, some may find the hierarchical nature of these organizations stifling and prefer a more flexible work environment. On the other hand, state employment offers stability, job security, and comprehensive benefits such as healthcare and retirement plans. Many Gen Z workers are drawn to the public sector due to its focus on serving the community and making a positive impact on society. Working for the government can provide a sense of purpose and fulfillment that may be lacking in other sectors. Alternatively, the Gig Economy appeals to Generation Z's desire for flexibility, autonomy, and work-life balance. Freelancing or working as an independent contractor allows individuals to choose their own projects, set their own schedules, and work from anywhere in the world. While this type of work can be unpredictable and lacks traditional benefits, it offers unparalleled freedom and the opportunity to pursue multiple interests simultaneously. Ultimately, you need to weigh the pros and cons of each work environment option based on your personal preferences, career goals, and values. Whatever you choose, it is important for you as a young professional to prioritize your well-being and long-term satisfaction in your chosen career path.

Ethics and environmental sustainability

When it comes to ethical decision-making and environmental sustainability, Generation Z is particularly conscientious and values-driven. They prioritize making choices that align with their ethical beliefs and contribute to a more sustainable future. Whether it's opting for eco-friendly products, supporting companies with transparent and ethical practices, or advocating for social and environmental causes, Gen Z is actively engaged in creating positive change. By considering the ethical implications of their decisions and striving to make environmentally sustainable choices, this generation is shaping a more responsible and socially conscious society for the future. Their commitment to ethics and sustainability sets a powerful example for generations to come.

Conclusion

Each area of life presents unique challenges and opportunities for decision-making. By approaching these decisions thoughtfully, mindfully, and intentionally, readers can navigate the complexities of life with confidence, clarity, and purpose.

3

The process of decision making

The process of decision-making is a fundamental aspect of human existence, shaping our actions, beliefs, and ultimately, our destinies. In the context of "Decisions for Generation Z: How to Choose in a World of Many Options," understanding and mastering the process of decision-making is essential for young individuals navigating the complexities of today's fast-paced world.

The decision-making process begins with identifying the need for a decision. Whether faced with a major life transition, a career dilemma, or a personal challenge, recognizing the need to make a choice is the first step towards taking control of one's life. This awareness sets the stage for deliberate and intentional decision-making.

Next, gathering information and evaluating options are crucial steps in the decision-making process. Researching alternatives, seeking advice from trusted sources, and weighing the pros and cons of each option can provide clarity and insight into the potential outcomes of different choices. In a world filled with endless possibilities, having a systematic approach to evaluating options can help individuals make informed decisions aligned with their values and goals.

Once options have been assessed, making a choice requires courage and conviction. Decision-making often involves stepping out of one's comfort zone, confronting uncertainty, and embracing change. By trusting in their judgment and intuition, individuals can make choices that resonate with their authentic selves and lead to personal growth and fulfillment.

After a decision has been made, taking action is essential to bring that choice to fruition. Implementing plans, setting goals, and staying committed to the chosen path are key components of turning decisions into reality. This phase requires perseverance, resilience, and adaptability as individuals navigate obstacles and challenges along the way.

Finally, reflecting on the outcomes of decisions is an important part of the process. Evaluating the results of choices made, learning from successes and failures, and adjusting course as needed are critical for ongoing personal growth and development. Reflection allows individuals to refine their decision-making skills, build resilience in the face of adversity, and continue evolving as empowered agents of their own lives.

The process of decision-making is a dynamic journey that empowers individuals to shape their destinies with intentionality and purpose. By understanding the steps involved in making choices, young people can navigate life's complexities with confidence, clarity, and resilience.

Tips and Tricks on How to Make Decisions

While decision-making can be challenging at times, there are several tips and tricks that can help individuals navigate the process with clarity and confidence. Here are some strategies to consider when faced with a decision:

Define your goals

Before making a decision, take the time to clarify your objectives and priorities. Understanding what you hope to achieve through your decision can provide a clear direction and guide your choices towards outcomes that align with your values and aspirations.

Gather information

Informed decisions are based on reliable information and insights. Take the time to research, gather data, and seek advice from trusted sources before making a choice. Consider the potential consequences of each option and weigh the pros and cons to make an informed decision.

Trust your intuition

While it's important to analyze information and consider different perspectives, don't underestimate the power of your intuition. Listen to your gut feelings, instincts, and inner wisdom when making decisions. Your intuition can often provide valuable insights that rational analysis may overlook.

Consider the long-term impact

When making decisions, think beyond immediate gratification or short-term gains. Consider how your choice will impact your future self, relationships, and goals. Evaluate the long-term consequences of each option to make decisions that are sustainable and aligned with your vision for the future.

Seek feedback

Don't hesitate to seek feedback from trusted friends, mentors, or advisors when making important decisions. Getting input from others can provide fresh perspectives, challenge assumptions, and help you see blind spots in your thinking. Consider diverse viewpoints before finalizing your decision.

Practice mindfulness

Cultivate mindfulness practices such as meditation, deep breathing, or grounding exercises to stay present and focused during the decision-making process. Mindfulness can help you tune into your thoughts, emotions, and intentions, allowing you to make decisions with clarity and awareness.

Embrace uncertainty

Accept that not all decisions will have clear-cut answers or guaranteed outcomes. Embrace uncertainty as a natural part of the decision-making process and be open to exploring different possibilities. Trust in your ability to adapt, learn from mistakes, and grow through experience.

Remember that decision-making is a skill that can be honed through practice, reflection, and continuous learning. May these strategies empower you to navigate decisions with grace and wisdom, leading you towards a future filled with purpose, fulfillment, and success.

Daily Decision

Daily decisions play a significant role in shaping our routines, habits, and overall well-being. While some decisions may seem small or routine, they can have a cumulative impact on our lives over time. Here follows a list of choices and decisions that you take every day, but might not be aware of:

- Morning and evening routine
- Time Management
- Healthy Eating
- Exercise
- Self-Care
- Financial Management
- Relationships
- Learning
- Sleep Routine
- Gratitude Practice
- and much more

Power of Habits

Habits are the invisible forces that shape our daily lives, influencing our thoughts, actions, and ultimately, our destinies. From the moment we wake up in the morning to the time we go to bed at night, habits dictate our routines, behaviors, and choices. The power of habits lies in their ability to create consistency, efficiency, and structure in our lives.

Developing positive habits can lead to personal growth, productivity, and overall well-being. Whether it's starting the day with a morning meditation, exercising regularly, or practicing gratitude before bedtime, cultivating healthy habits can have a transformative impact on our mental, emotional, and physical health.

On the other hand, breaking negative habits requires awareness, intentionality, and perseverance. Whether it's overcoming procrastination, reducing screen time, or quitting unhealthy vices, changing ingrained behaviors can be challenging but ultimately rewarding. By replacing destructive habits with constructive ones, we can unlock our full potential and create a life filled with purpose, fulfillment, and success.

In essence, the power of habits lies in their ability to shape our identities and influence our outcomes. By harnessing the power of habits consciously and intentionally, we can cultivate a lifestyle that aligns with our values, goals, and aspirations – leading to a life of meaning, joy, and fulfillment.

Thinking Outside the Box

> When I decided to leave the country, that was a step which was outside of the box. No one in my family made this before. In fact I did not know many people personally that made this step. So it was a step in faith not knowing what will happen. But this step made me experience life changing moments and defined very much who I am today. So it was really

worth it and I would strongly recommend thinking outside the box.

"Thinking outside the box" is a mindset that encourages creativity, innovation and unconventional approaches to problem-solving and decision-making. When individuals think outside the box, they challenge traditional norms, explore new possibilities, and consider alternative perspectives that may lead to unique solutions. In the context of decision-making, thinking outside the box can be a valuable approach to generating fresh ideas, overcoming obstacles, and making bold choices. Here are some ways in which thinking outside the box can enhance decision-making:

- Exploring Unconventional Solutions
- Embracing Creativity
- Seeking Diverse Perspectives
- Taking Calculated Risks
- Encouraging Collaboration
- Questioning Assumptions
- Fostering Curiosity
- Experimenting with Prototyping:

Remember that thinking outside the box is not about abandoning logic or reason but rather expanding your perspective, considering new possibilities and challenging yourself to approach decisions with creativity and courage. By embracing this mindset you can unlock your full potential as a decision-maker and navigate challenges with confidence and clarity vision.

4

Obstacles

When I decided to go and live in another country, I started to communicate it to my friends and family. Obviously, not everyone was amazed about my choice. This was an obstacle for me. I had to experience questioning, doubts, and incomprehension which led me to question my decision. Was it really the right decision? But it was actually very important to overcome these obstacles and ultimately showed me that I was on the right path. Yes, that's exactly what I wanted, to live in another country for once.

D ecision-making is a complex process that involves weighing options, considering consequences, and choosing a course of action. While making decisions is a fundamental aspect of daily life, various obstacles can hinder the process and lead to indecision, uncertainty, and regret. In this chapter, we will explore common obstacles in decision-making and provide strategies for overcoming them to enhance focus, productivity, and personal growth.

Overcoming the Paralysis of Infinite Choice Online

In today's digital age, the abundance of information and options available online can overwhelm individuals and lead to decision paralysis. The constant barrage of choices on social media, e-commerce platforms, and search engines can make it challenging to make informed decisions. To overcome the paralysis of infinite choice online, consider the following strategies:

Set clear goals

Define your objectives and priorities before engaging with online content or making decisions. Having a clear sense of purpose can help you filter out irrelevant information and focus on what truly matters to you.

Limit information overload

Be selective about the sources of information you consume online. Avoid getting caught up in endless scrolling or comparison shopping by setting boundaries on your screen time and prioritizing quality over quantity.

Practice mindfulness

Cultivate awareness of your thoughts and emotions while browsing online. Mindfulness techniques such as deep breathing, meditation, or grounding exercises can help you stay present and focused amidst distractions.

Seek trusted sources

When seeking information or advice online, prioritize reputable sources and experts in the relevant field. Verify the credibility of sources before making decisions based on their recommendations.

By implementing these strategies, you can navigate the overwhelming landscape of online choices more effectively and make decisions that align with your values and goals.

Techniques to Enhance Focus and Productivity:

Maintaining focus and productivity is essential for effective decision-making and achieving desired outcomes. However, distractions, multitasking, and procrastination can impede progress and hinder decision clarity. To enhance focus and productivity, consider incorporating the following techniques into your daily routine:

Time blocking

Allocate specific blocks of time for focused work on important tasks or decision-making activities. By creating dedicated time slots for specific activities, you can minimize distractions and maximize productivity.

Prioritize tasks

Identify high-priority tasks that require immediate attention or have significant impact on your goals. Use tools such as task lists, calendars, or project management software to organize tasks based on urgency and importance.

Break tasks into smaller steps

Divide complex decisions or projects into smaller manageable steps to avoid feeling overwhelmed. By breaking down tasks into actionable items, you can make progress incrementally and maintain momentum towards your goals.

Eliminate distractions

Minimize external distractions such as notifications, noise, or clutter in your environment to create a conducive space for focused work. Consider using noise-canceling headphones, setting boundaries with colleagues or family members, or decluttering your workspace to enhance concentration.

By incorporating these techniques into your daily routine, you can improve focus, increase productivity, and make informed decisions with clarity and confidence.

Escaping the Comparison Trap

Comparing oneself to others is a common obstacle that can undermine self-confidence, create feelings of inadequacy, and lead to poor decision-making. The prevalence of social media and constant exposure to curated images of success can fuel the comparison trap, making it difficult to stay true to one's values and aspirations. To escape the comparison trap, consider the following strategies:

- Cultivate self-awareness

- Practice gratitude
- Set realistic goals
- Limit social media exposure
- Seek to help others, instead of comparing yourself to them

Lifelong Learning

Embracing lifelong learning is essential for personal growth, professional development, and effective decision-making. Continuous learning allows individuals to expand their knowledge base, acquire new skills, and adapt to changing circumstances in an ever-evolving world. To cultivate a mindset of lifelong learning, consider the following strategies:

- Pursue formal and informal education
- Read widely and as much as you can
- Seek mentorship
- Experiment and iterate
- Try new activities
- Explore different interests
- Take calculated risks

Privacy in the Digital Age - Safeguarding Your Online Identity

In today's interconnected world, where technology plays a central role in our daily lives, safeguarding your online identity and privacy has become more important than ever. With the vast amount of personal information shared online, it is crucial to take proactive steps to protect your data from potential threats and breaches. This chapter explores key strategies and best practices for maintaining privacy in the digital age.

Understand Your Digital Footprint

Your digital footprint consists of all the information about you that is available online. This includes social media profiles, browsing history, online purchases, and more. Understanding the extent of your digital footprint is the first step towards safeguarding your online identity.

Use Strong Passwords

One of the simplest yet most effective ways to protect your online accounts is by using strong, unique passwords for each account. Avoid using easily guessable passwords and consider using a password manager to securely store and manage your passwords.

Enable Two-Factor Authentication

Two-factor authentication adds an extra layer of security to your accounts by requiring a second form of verification, such as a code sent to your phone or email. Enable two-factor authentication whenever possible to enhance the security of your online accounts.

Be Mindful of What You Share

Think twice before sharing personal information online, especially on social media platforms. Be cautious about sharing sensitive details such as your address, phone number, or financial information, as this information can be used by malicious actors for identity theft or fraud.

Review Privacy Settings

Regularly review the privacy settings on your social media accounts, apps, and devices to ensure that you are comfortable with the level of information being shared. Adjust settings to limit who can see your posts, photos, and personal details.

Update Software Regularly

Keep your devices and software up to date with the latest security patches and updates. Outdated software can be vulnerable to cyber attacks, so staying current with updates is essential for protecting your data.

Use Secure Wi-Fi Networks

When accessing the internet on public Wi-Fi networks, be cautious about sharing sensitive information such as passwords or financial details. Use virtual private networks (VPNs) to encrypt your connection and add an extra layer of security.

Monitor Your Accounts

Regularly monitor your bank accounts, credit reports, and online transactions for any suspicious activity. Report any unauthorized charges or unusual behavior immediately to prevent further damage to your online identity.

    I strongly recommend you to think about your online identity and take proactive steps to protect your personal information and privacy in this digital age. Remember that maintaining privacy requires ongoing vigilance, awareness, and a commitment to staying informed about emerging threats and security measures. Stay informed, stay vigilant, and stay safe in an increasingly connected world where privacy matters more than ever before.

Conclusion

Resuming this chapter please note that obstacles in any form or shape will come. The question is not if, but when. They will arise and mostly when you don't expect them. This is why we had to discuss the topic in this chapter. As long as you know that obstacles, questions and doubt are part of the process, you are ahead of the game.

5

How to communicate your decision

Communication is a vital skill that influences how we express our thoughts, feelings, and decisions to ourselves and others. Effectively conveying our decisions is essential for clarity, understanding, and building strong relationships. Whether it's communicating a personal choice to oneself or sharing a decision with others, mastering the art of communication can lead to positive outcomes and meaningful connections.

Communicating Decisions to Yourself:

Self-communication plays a crucial role in the decision-making process, as it involves reflecting on choices, understanding motivations, and aligning actions with values. To effectively communicate decisions to yourself, consider the following strategies:

Self-reflection

Take time to introspect and evaluate the reasons behind your decision. Ask yourself questions about your goals, priorities, and values to gain clarity on why you made a particular choice.

Positive self-talk

Use affirmations and positive language to reinforce your decision and boost your confidence. Remind yourself of your strengths, capabilities, and resilience in facing the consequences of your choice.

Visualization

Picture yourself implementing your decision successfully and imagine the positive outcomes that may result from it. Visualizing the desired end result can motivate you to stay committed to your decision.

Journaling

Write down your thoughts, emotions, and reflections on the decision-making process. Keeping a journal can help you track your progress, identify patterns in your decision-making behavior, and gain insights into your thought processes.

By engaging in effective self-communication practices, you can strengthen your self-awareness, enhance your decision-making skills, and cultivate a deeper understanding of yourself.

Communicating Decisions to Others:

Sharing decisions with others requires empathy, clarity, and effective communication skills to ensure mutual understanding and respect. Here are some tips for communicating decisions to others:

Active listening

Before conveying your decision, listen attentively to the perspectives and concerns of others involved. Show empathy and understanding towards their viewpoints before expressing your own stance.

Clarity and transparency

Clearly articulate the reasons behind your decision, including any relevant information or factors that influenced your choice. Be transparent about your intentions and objectives to build trust and credibility.

Respectful dialogue

Engage in open and respectful communication with others, allowing space for differing opinions and perspectives. Encourage constructive feedback and dialogue to foster mutual understanding and collaboration.

Setting boundaries

Clearly define boundaries around your decision to establish expectations and prevent misunderstandings. Communicate any limitations or constraints related to your choice while respecting the boundaries of others involved.

By practicing effective communication skills when sharing decisions with others, you can promote harmonious relationships, build trust, and navigate conflicts constructively.

Conclusion

Mastering the art of communicating decisions – both to oneself and to others – is essential for personal growth, interpersonal relationships, and effective decision-making. Effective communication fosters understanding, empowers individuals to assert their choices with conviction and builds strong connections based on trust and mutual respect. Ultimately, the ability to communicate decisions effectively is a valuable skill that contributes to personal fulfillment, harmonious relationships, and successful outcomes in all areas of life.

6

Conclusion

We have seen in this short little book that there are many important choices and decisions in life. We saw that there is power in a decision. As long as you didn't take a decision (which is also a decision) there is no further step possible. So, we strongly recommend that you take it seriously and make decisions in our daily life. Because:

> **The decision of today, makes the you of tomorrow**

We talked about the decision making process and how we spent a great deal of time considering the obstacles. And here is what we found out:

> **As long as you know that obstacles, questions and doubt are part of the process, you are ahead of the game.**

Now it's up to you, to make decisions and start to communicate them and see the results and the happiness that will come out of it.

Yes, I hope that you can have the same experiences that I had many, many times in life. A good decision gives so much power and joy, you cannot imagine it, as long as you have not experienced it. And a bad decision is even better than no decision at all. Because you will find out that it was wrong and you can correct, adapt and go on to the next destination. I would love to hear about your experiences that you made with good and bad decisions. Please write me a favorable review on Amazon and maybe, I will see you on a gate boarding a plane, because you made a decision.

www.ingramcontent.com/pod-product-compliance
Lightning Source LLC
Chambersburg PA
CBHW072056230526
45479CB00010B/1100